Fifty Footballing

G000153441

Kevin McCann

Kevin was born in Blackpool and has supported his home town team all his life through thick and thin – and there's been a lot of thin. Most seasons see them on the crest of another slump.

Harry Potter creator JK Rowling said she had met people who didn't want to try for fear of failing. When it comes to muck-ups some football clubs, players, managers and match officials don't have to try. For them muck-ups occur quite naturally and sometimes quite often.

Footballing muck-ups are not a stranger to Blackpool supporters, nor are they a stranger to other football fans.

Here are *Fifty Footballing Muck-ups...*

1. THAT WAS QUICK!

Uruguay boasts a record for the fastest sending off in a World Cup finals game. Just 56 seconds against a disappointing (no surprises there) Scotland (played three, won none) in 1986. Beat that!

Well, it can be beaten. Sheffield Wednesday's goalkeeper Kevin Pressman lasted only 13 seconds in the first match of the new season in 2000. Playing at the Molineux Stadium, home of Wolverhampton Wanderers, Pressman did what keepers were meant to do: diving and using his hands to clear the ball. Unfortunately, he hadn't received the memo about not doing it outside the penalty area. He was given a straight red. Beat that!

Well, Swansea centre forward Walter Boyd can. Manager John Hollins took advantage of a free kick to bring on substitute Boyd. But before the ref could restart the game, his attention was drawn to a Darlington player, Martin Gray, who was lying face down on the floor. The assistant ref informed his colleague that Boyd had elbowed Gray in the head. So, after being on the pitch for zero seconds of the actual match, Boyd received his marching orders. Beat that!

Actually, it can be beaten. Ian Banks of Barnsley was warming up prior to making an appearance as a substitute and was sent off before he came on. In the match against Bournemouth he received a straight red for suggesting to the referee's assistant, with hindsight a touch too forcibly, that a decision made was perhaps incorrect. Beat that!

Incredibly, Patrice Evra can. Playing for Marseille against Vitoria SC he was sent off for trying to kick a supporter, as you do, before the game had started.

Now that will really take some beating!

2.EARLY TO BED, EARLY TO RISE

Queens Park Rangers defender Bob Malcolm, on loan from Derby County, must have had a particularly tough match at Plymouth the previous day as he was found asleep. Nothing too much to worry about there – having a post-match nap is not unusual. Having said that, it was in the driving seat of his car. Nothing to worry about there then; after all, it must have been a long drive home from Plymouth and 90 minutes of football can be very tiring. However, and this is where things escalate very swiftly, he was parked in the middle lane of the M1. It will astonish no one that he subsequently failed a breath test and was banned from driving for 20 months.

Malcolm does have previous. In mid-2004 a warrant was issued for Malcolm's arrest after he failed to appear in court on a speeding charge, for which he was later fined £250.

Malcolm also has previous, previous (if you see what I mean), as before that he was fined £5,000 by his then club Glasgow Rangers for writing FTP (short hand for F**K the Pope) when asked for his autograph.

3.ODD INJURIES

There have been some high-profile odd injuries. David Beckham requiring stitches after being hit by a flying boot kicked by Alex Ferguson during an animated team talk, and Steve Morrow breaking his collar bone falling off Tony Adams shoulders when celebrating a League Cup victory are well known examples. Others are less well chronicled.

Goalkeeper Vince Bartram's career was finished in a goal-mouth collision which resulted in a badly fractured wrist. Tragic, you might think, but the sort of thing that can happen to keepers. Well, this collision was with the opposition keeper who had come up for a last-minute corner.

Brentford keeper, Chic Brodie, also had his career finished by a collision – with a dog which had run onto the pitch. Desperately bad news for Chic, but there was some good news … the dog was okay.

The ex-Wimbledon (but by then Chelsea) keeper Dave Beasant once fumbled a four-pound jar of salad cream, put his foot out to stop it crashing to the floor and severed tendons. Two months out injured. Who would have thought a goalie would drop something?

Darren Barnard of Barnsley slipped in a puddle of his new puppy's pee and was out of action for five months with knee ligament damage. It was a good job he didn't have a pet elephant.

Arsenal's Perry Groves was a substitute sitting in the dugout. Arsenal scored, and you can almost picture what happened next. Groves jumped up in excitement, hit his head on the roof and knocked himself out. This episode never made it to 'What Happened Next' on *A Question of Sport* but it should have done.

One odd injury that would not have made it on to *A Question of Sport* would have been Brazilian international

Ramalho's unfortunate error. Ramalho was confined to bed after swallowing a suppository. It makes you wonder what he did with his toothbrush.

4. ROLY-POLY GOALIE

It was a big day for Sutton United of the National League; they were playing Arsenal in the FA Cup at home. The attention of the national media was on little Sutton; it was their chance to bask in impossible-to-buy publicity, if only for 90 minutes. It was a shame that it wasn't for footballing reasons that Sutton made headlines.

Their reserve goalkeeper, Wayne Shaw, weighed in at an impressive 23 stones and is, unsurprisingly, nicknamed the roly-poly goalie. Probably as homage to the popular chant of 'Who ate all the pies?', a leading bookmaker offered odds that Wayne would actually eat a pie live on TV during the match. As he sat on the substitutes' bench, that is exactly what happened. There was Wayne, on TV, eating a pie.

To be clear, the roly-poly goalie didn't bet himself – that would have been stupid. Although I'm sure that, with the aid of hindsight, Wayne now realises eating a pie on national TV in the middle of the match is erring towards stupidity.

The result? Wayne resigned and left Sutton United. Oh, that result. Arsenal won 2–0.

There is a subsequent twist. In the very next game, Sutton's first-choice keeper was injured during the game and had to be replaced by an outfield player because they hadn't signed a replacement for Wayne.

5. I WON'T KEEP YOU LONG

Artist Andy Warhol is quoted as saying, 'In the future, everybody will be famous for fifteen minutes.' For Leroy Rosenior, it was actually ten minutes.

Rosenior was a striker who spent nearly all his career with London clubs. He played for Queens Park Rangers, West Ham United, Fulham and Charlton Athletic before ending his professional career in that far-flung place known as Bristol City – well, given his London-centric career, it was far flung for Leroy. He also won one international cap for Sierra Leone, but failed to score in the match against Togo, a no score bore draw.

Following his playing career, Rosenior served his apprenticeship as a manager and coach with non-league teams before leading Bristol City reserves and then being appointed the manager at Torquay. He successfully got them promoted back into League One but the success was short lived and he left by mutual consent after relegation and then only three wins the following season back in League Two. But he must have left on good terms as just over a year later he was back as manager at Torquay.

The first stint as manager at the Gulls was three-and-a-half years. The second stint didn't last quite as long: ten minutes, to be precise. He started the 'welcome to the new manager' press conference as the manager at Plainmoor and by the end of the interview he was their ex-manager. In between the start and finish of the press conference, a local consortium had bought the club and immediately appointed Paul Buckle as manager instead.

Leroy was subsequently at the forefront of anti-racism campaigns headed by the organisation, Show Racism the Red Card, and he was awarded the MBE for his work in addressing discrimination. But for many, his biggest claim to fame lasted just ten minutes.

6

6. DON'T OVERDO IT

Kevin Keegan, the then Messiah (sorry, manager) at Newcastle, signed goalkeeper Mike Hooper from Liverpool for £550,000. This was not an inconsiderable sum in the early 1990s, especially for someone who didn't play very often. Hooper's eight years on Merseyside saw him make just 51 appearances, averaging about six games a season. During his three years at Newcastle he had to make more of an effort on match days, but he can hardly be described as prolific: he appeared in 25 games, approximately eight games a season. Hooper did have a spell on loan to Sunderland, but you won't be surprised to hear that he failed to make a single appearance. He retired after twelve years in football with 125 appearances.

He does have a first-class honours degree in English Literature from Swansea University, where he is ranked number 18 on their famous alumni list, one place behind historian John Latimer. No, me neither.

7. THE DELTIOLOGIST

Deltiology relates to the collection of red and yellow cards. Actually, it relates to the collection of postcards but I couldn't find a term for a footballer who collects red and yellow cards. If there was one, then it would certainly apply to Lee Cattermole.

Lee was appointed captain at Sunderland by manager Steve Bruce ahead of the 2010/11 season. After the first four matches he had been sent off twice, including a dismissal on the first day of the season. The following season saw a slightly improved attitude, with only two yellows in the first two games.

Lee reached a milestone in 2015/16 when he achieved a total of 100 yellow cards to go with his eight sendings-off in just ten years. By the way, for reasons I cannot fathom, he was no longer captain.

Off the pitch he has form, though not footballing form. He has been banned from every pub in Stockton and given a caution for damage to cars after a night out in Newcastle.

He has been described as a defensive midfielder. With, at the last count, 119 yellows and nine reds in total, I'd call him anything but defensive.

8. IT'S ONLY THE CHAIRBOYS

Premier League Leicester City's 2001 march to FA Cup immortality looked like a formality when they were drawn at home to Division 2 team Wycombe Wanderers (nicknamed the Chairboys) in the quarter finals. Leicester must have really fancied their chances when the draw was made, especially in the week before the tie when Wycombe put an advert for a striker on Ceefax. With all their forwards at the club injured and none fit to play in their biggest game ever, the Chairboys were desperate to find a fit, non-Cup tied attacker.

Step forward Roy Essandoh. Actually, it was Essandoh's agent who stepped forward, but you get the drift. Roy's CV wasn't exactly impressive for a centre forward: 12 goals in 81 games and they had all come in Finland's Second Division. No disrespect to Finland's Second Division but, once again, you get my drift. The romance of the FA Cup was enhanced as Essandoh was named as a substitute.

Leicester must have had their eyes on a semi-final place. Initially supremely confident, Leicester were no doubt a bit jittery after a goalless first half. They got even more jittery after 50 minutes, when Wycombe defender Paul McCarthy scored. Those jitters were calmed when Muzzy Izzet equalised ten minutes later.

With fifteen minutes to go, Essandoh entered the match. With a replay beckoning in time added on, his and Wycombe's dream came true. He scored. The Chairboys were in the semi-final of the FA Cup and top-flight Leicester could not quite comprehend what had happened.

Leicester made FA Cup history for all the wrong reasons and Wycombe for all the right ones, although The Chairboys ultimately lost to Liverpool in the semi-final.

As for Roy Essandoh, he left Wycombe at the end of the season and moved into a nomadic non-league career. Not quite the happy ending he and his agent might have hoped for.

9. SUPER SUBS

It is important for footballers to know that they have the confidence of their manager. They want to be one of the first names on the team sheet, an automatic selection. Some are automatic selections, but do not appear in the first eleven. This is the group of players who carve out a career as substitutes. The elite few become super subs.

Arguably, the most successful substitute is – big drum roll please – Ole Gunnar Solskjaer! The Norwegian striker, who scored as a super sub in injury-time of the 1999 European Cup Final, scored 29 of his 126 goals at Manchester United after coming off the bench. His first goal for United came six minutes after he was introduced in a home match against Blackburn Rovers. Incredibly, his last goal for United also came six minutes after he came off the bench at home to Blackburn Rovers. Spooky!

His nearest rival, Liverpool's David Fairclough, scored a very creditable 18 of his 55 goals as a substitute during his time at Anfield.

Perhaps the term 'super sub' can also be bestowed on the Republic of Ireland's Tony Cascarino, who scored 19 times in 88 international appearances, 48 of them as a substitute. Nice work if you can get it.

Having said all that, even the best super subs didn't convince their manager that they were worth a regular starting place. 'Super sub' is a label that suggests you are not quite good enough for the first eleven.

10. THAT'S NOT VERY FRIENDLY

Of course, some would say that there is no such thing as a friendly match in football. As Liverpool manager Bill Shankly once said, 'They say football's a matter of life and death – but it's more important than that.'

On April 1st – I kid you not – 1997, Jamaica played Mexico's Toros Neza. The friendly (I use that word advisedly) was to help the Jamaicans acclimatise to playing at altitude ahead of their World Cup qualifier against Mexico.

After twenty minutes of what can best be described as getting your retaliation in first, fighting broke out between the two teams. Jamaica then decided to take a firmer line; they left the pitch only to return fully armed with broken bottles, bricks and a chair (obviously). The match officials made a sharp exit.

The match was abandoned, but you had probably worked that out already. The World Cup match against Mexico? A six-goal thriller. Mexico 6, Jamaica 0.

11. THE MIGHTY ROBINS

You'll find this hard to believe, but in 1970 Swindon (sometimes, but not very often, called the Mighty Robins) took on Napoli (yes, *that* Napoli) in the Anglo-Italian Cup. The Anglo-Italian Cup ran intermittently in the 1970s, 1980s and 1990s. The reasons for the matches were no doubt financial, but there was also a desire to see English teams take on Italian teams in a competitive environment. And the first final between the Mighty Robins and Napoli was certainly competitive.

Fifty thousand Napoli fans, who had already staged two pitch invasions before Swindon took a 3–0 lead on the hour, decided that if their team couldn't stop the pride of Wiltshire, they would. Once again they invaded the pitch, this time using seats, bottles and rocks to attack the Swindon players and the match officials. The police decided that it might be an idea to do something, so they fired tear gas and a full-scale riot followed.

Swindon, to the surprise of not many, were awarded the game and Napoli, to the surprise of not many, were suspended from European football for two years.

12. THAT'S A RELIEF

If there was an award for the most unusual sending off, it would surely go to Premier League goalkeeper Scott O'Rourke. I say 'Premier League'; that's the Wessex Premier League.

O'Rourke played for Hampshire side Brockenhurst. He was dismissed for ungentlemanly conduct. 'Ungentlemanly conduct?' I hear you ask. He had a pee behind the goal as the match was being played.

The crowd were probably appalled and embarrassed in equal measures. I say 'crowd', but that's a bit of poetic licence on my part as there were less than 100 spectators 'packed' (poetic licence again) into Brockenhurst's Grigg Lane ground.

O'Rourke and Brockenhurst also made it into the record books for their marathon penalty shoot-out with Andover Town in the Hampshire Senior Cup. Nil–nil after 90 minutes and extra time, the penalty shoot-out went on … and on … and on … and on. Twenty-nine consecutive penalties were scored before O'Rourke became the hero and saved the thirtieth spot kick.

In fairness to O'Rourke, he had the modesty to point out that he let 14 penalties in before making that save.

13. WHAT SEEMS TO BE THE PROBLEM?

You can picture the scene. The doctor says to the player, 'How did this happen? In training? An awkward fall on match day? Bad tackle?' Some players have to give an embarrassed cough and explain what actually happened.

Clumsy keeper Santiago Canizares fumbled a bottle of aftershave which crashed to the floor. A stray piece of glass from the bottle severed a tendon in his toe, forcing him to miss the 2002 World Cup. He did play for Spain in three other World Cups though and earlier in his career won a gold medal in the 1992 Olympics. Off the field Canizares wasn't exactly idle. He is father of seven children, including triplets, and took up rally driving when his time in football came to an end.

Norwegian international Svein Grondalen missed a match in the 1970s after colliding with a moose while out jogging. To confirm, that is definitely a moose and not a mouse.

And talking of tiny animals, Leeds midfielder David Batty suffered a relapse of an old Achilles tendon problem when his toddler rode into the back of his ankle on a tricycle.

Kevin Kyle, then at Sunderland, was preparing to feed his baby when the youngster knocked over a jug of boiling water Kyle was using to warm a bottle into his father's lap. The big striker spent a night in hospital with very sore testicles.

Kids, eh? Who'd have them? Probably not Kevin Kyle. Not for a long, long time. Perhaps never again.

14. ROVERS TO RANGERS

It was Scottish legend Jock Stein who said that football was nothing without fans. Gretna went even further and showed that football is nothing without a team.

Gretna is best known for two reasons: runaway marriages, and the meteoric rise of its football team from English non-league to Scottish Premier. Actually, it's Gretna Green that is associated with eloping couples, but the football club definitely went from playing Gresley Rovers to Glasgow Rangers. Then it went bust.

Promoted from the Northern League to the Northern Premier First Division in the 1980s, the Northern Premier Division in the 90s and the Scottish League in 2002, Gretna hit the big time. They surged through the Scottish Third Division with a record of 13 straight wins. The surge continued through the Second Division, when they lost only four times. Imagine the scenes as they made it out of the First Division with a last-minute goal in the last game of the season.

However, managing director Brooks Mileson's millions were no guarantee of success in the Premier Division and Gretna faced a stiff reality check. The small Raydale Park stadium did not meet Scottish Premier League requirements, so Gretna faced a 150-mile round trip to play 'home' games at Motherwell. With average home gates struggling to reach 1,500 other than when the big two Glasgow clubs visited, home games 75 miles away proved football is nothing without fans.

By the end of the season, they were in administration after an ailing Mileson had withdrawn his support. Gretna had creditors of nearly £4m and assets of less than £1m. By the start of the following season, they had formally gone out of business. Sadly, Mileson died shortly afterwards and for Gretna fans football was nothing without a team.

15. THE IMPORTANCE OF REHYDRATION

Qualifying for the 2010 World Cup was always going to be a difficult task for Scotland as only the group winners had automatic qualification; runners up have to try again via play-offs. And Holland were in the same group as Scotland.

Following a 3–0 demolition by the Dutch in Amsterdam, the home match versus Iceland a few days later took on huge significance. Scotland needed to win; to secure the runners-up spot, they needed to win convincingly and boost their goal difference.

The build-up to the game was completely undermined by Barry Ferguson and Allan McGregor. Instead of heading off to bed on their return from Amsterdam, they went to the bar for a late-night, early-morning, late-morning drinking session in the team hotel.

Manager George Burley dropped the two of them but, for reasons he probably regrets to this day, he let the errant players stay with the squad and join their colleagues on the bench for the all-important game.

Most people would have kept an embarrassed silence and a low profile. Not these two. The players were snapped making V-signs to photographers during the match. Ferguson was stripped of the captaincy of Rangers and sold to Birmingham City. Whatever your wrongdoing, being sold to Birmingham City seems a bit harsh. McGregor, although still at Rangers, wasn't picked again that season as the Glasgow club clinched a domestic double.

Both were banned for life from representing Scotland, although goalkeeper McGregor did return the following season. Clearly life expectancy is a few months for the Scottish FA.

Qualification for the World Cup? Scotland could only scrape a 2–1 win against Iceland, who finished bottom of the group. Norway finished ahead of Scotland on goal difference to claim the runners-up spot.

16. RESERVATION FOR BEAGRIE

Perhaps the prize for the most bizarre drink-induced stunt goes to the nomadic, ten-clubs winger Peter Beagrie. Wait for the punch line at the end.

In 1991 Beagrie, then at Everton, was enjoying a pre-season, post-match session (drinking, not training) when he decided it was time to go back to the hotel. Very sensible. He hitched a lift back on the back of a motorcycle. Less sensible. When the night porter couldn't be located to let him in, Beagrie drove the motorcycle up the hotel steps and through a large window. Not at all sensible, particularly as he required 50 stitches.

As promised, here comes the punch line. It was the wrong hotel.

17. TOUCH WOOD

Research at a leading German university demonstrated that there was a correlation between adhering to pre-match superstition and the eventual result. It would seem that sticking to your superstitions ensures you win matches. Actually, I just made that up. Of course walking down the tunnel last or sitting in the same place in a dressing room doesn't mean you will win a game. Who would be daft enough to think so?

The usually nailed-on certainties for a semi – if not a final – place, the German team refused to stay on the thirteenth floor of their hotel in Euro 2004. The hotel management agreed to the German's request to be moved off the unlucky floor.

Despite not being on the thirteenth floor, Germany failed to win a single match and went out in the group stages. It would seem performances on the pitch are more important than superstition off the pitch.

18. UNLUCKY BLACK CATS

Sunderland (aka the Black Cats) were relegated from the Premier League in 2003 with a then record low of just four wins, 19 points and 21 goals from 38 games. When you think about it, it really is hard to be that bad. That is not to say there was a goal drought when Sunderland played; thank goodness for the opposing teams, who put away 65 goals.

However, what followed was good news, bad news, good news and then OK news for the Black Cats – before bad news once again.

The good news is that they bounced back to the Premier Division in 2005. The bad news is that they were relegated back to the Championship the following season in 2006. Their leading goal scorer that season had three league goals and this time they only managed three wins and 15 points. The next good news is that they immediately regained their place in the top flight. OK news might be an apt description of what followed. The next decade saw them finish in the top half of the league once – and that was tenth out of twenty. Even the FA Cup offered little respite, going out in Round 3 on five out of ten occasions.

It perhaps comes as no surprise that Sunderland were relegated in 2017, although in that year they did win six games and scored a dazzling 29 goals. They only had one season in the Championship though – but that was because they were relegated the very next season.

Bad times make the good times even better. Try telling that to a Sunderland fan.

19. ALWAYS SOMETHING TO PLAY FOR

Expectation and reality could be so different, particularly for West Bromwich Albion supporters in the noughties.

When the Baggies won promotion to the Premiership in 2002, expectations must have been sky high. A large dose of reality soon followed when they were relegated in 2003. Expectations rose when they were promoted again in 2004, and things were marginally better as they avoided the drop on the last day of the 2005 season. Once again reality triumphed over expectation the following season: in 2006 they were down again. In 2007 they lost at Wembley to Derby in the play-offs. In 2008 they were back in the Premier Division, only to be relegated again to start 2009 in the Championship. And in 2010? Yes, back to the Premier Division.

Since then? Well, 2013 was a high point with an eighth-place finish but 2018 saw them go down again. We can only guess what ups and downs, quite literally, face Baggies fans in the 2020s.

20. A HANDY PLAYER

The England team's performance after the 1966 triumph could best be described as 'could do better' and perhaps, more honestly, as poor. They qualified for Mexico in 1970 as reigning champions but then failed to qualify for the 1974 and 1978 finals. In 1982, for the first time the top two teams from each qualifying group went to the finals held in Spain; England could count their blessings as they finished runners up to Hungary. England went home without scoring a goal in the second group stage.

And then it was back to Mexico in '86. England topped their qualifying group and expectations were high. True, things didn't start well when they lost to Portugal 1–0, before drawing 0–0 with Morocco. At that point the team needed a hero to step up and guarantee England what everyone *'Back Home'* (see what I did there with the 1970 team song?) saw as their rightful place in the second stage. A first half hat-trick from Gary Lineker made sure Poland were overwhelmed. In the last 16, two more goals from Lineker and one from Peter Beardsley were enough to see off Paraguay.

And so, it was the quarter finals and Argentina. The first forty-five minutes ended with no score. Something special and remarkable was going to be needed to break the deadlock – and we certainly got it. And we got it twice: once though the infamous Maradona 'Hand of God', and once through the exceptional Maradona dribble that beat several English players, including Terry Butcher, twice.

Gary Lineker did pull one back but the result was a 2–1 defeat. The good news was that Lineker got the golden boot award for the top scorer in the competition. I'm sure that thrilled everyone *'Back Home'* (see, I did it again).

Incidentally, the team song in 1986 was co-written by Tony Hiller who also wrote a string of hits for the

Brotherhood of Man. No, I wasn't aware the Brotherhood of Man had enjoyed a string of hits either. A bit like the team's performance, the record flattered to deceive and the unforgettable *'We've Got the Whole World at Our Feet'* peaked at 66. A bit like the England football team, really.

21. DON'T MAKE THINGS WORSE THAN THEY ALREADY ARE

Sheffield Wednesday midfielder Jermaine Johnson had been substituted in a stormy Steel City derby. It is doubtless an understatement to say he was a little disappointed. Just as he was about to have a shower, he was summoned back to the pitch side by referee Mike Dean. Dressed in vest and shorts, Johnson was given a yellow card for having kicked a water bottle into the crowd, and then a red card for pushing and shoving members of his own coaching staff during his first march off down the tunnel.

Johnson made his way politely down the tunnel for a second time, apologising profusely to all concerned.

I might be wrong about the politely bit. And the apology bit.

22. HOW MANY GOALKEEPERS DOES IT TAKE TO SAVE A PENALTY?

It is true to say that not many football fans would have been following the Northern Premier League clash between Guiseley and Hednesford Town, but those who did saw a world record. Almost.

Having taken an early lead, Guiseley had goalkeeper Piotr Skiba shown a straight red card after his outstretched arm 'came into contact' with an opponent. I think we can all picture what happened.

Guiseley substituted an outfield player to bring reserve keeper Aaron Ratchford off the bench to replace Skiba. Before he could actually face the penalty Ratchford, who was making his first team debut, was shown a yellow card for committing the outrageous crime of standing behind the goal line. Hednesford eventually put the penalty away.

With a minute of remaining normal time, a Hednesford player went down in the area as Ratchford raced out to smother the ball at his feet. The keeper received a second yellow card for that offence and then red for two bookings.

Guiseley didn't have a third keeper in their match-day squad (rubbish team selection) so midfielder David Briggs took the gloves. Some – admittedly not many and perhaps no one –knew that another goalkeeper sent off would lead to a world-record-breaking three goalkeepers dismissed in one game! It didn't happen, and history wasn't made. The penalty was missed and the referee blew for full time.

Oh, and Guiseley lost 2–1. But the memories of the controversial match live on. In parts of Guiseley, anyway.

23. NEW SEASON, NEW KIT

New season, new kit. It's a big money earner.

Once upon a time, clubs had two kits: a 'first-choice kit' used most of the time, and a 'change kit' for use on the rare occasions when there was a clash of colours with the opposition. Nowadays teams have home, away, third-choice and even special occasion strips.

In the 1970s, Coventry City (the Sky Blues) decided that the change strip would be ... brown! I know it was the decade when flares, kipper ties and paisley shirts were the ultimate fashion statement. But brown?

Ross County have a tartan strip, which has been relegated from their official away kit to one that only gets worn for special occasions. Luckily Ross County don't have many special occasions.

Brighton and Hove Albion combined blue-and-white striped shirts – okay so far – with blue-and-white striped shorts. Not okay. It gave the impression of deckchairs, or a team in striped pyjamas, running up and down the pitch.

In the early seventies, York City played in maroon shirts with a big white Y. Two years later the boffins in the design department surpassed themselves by coming up with white shirts and a big maroon Y. And you'll never guess what the kit was nicknamed. Oh, you did? Yes, it was known as the 'Y-front kit'.

24. FIFA's FOLLY?

Cameroon had their comeuppance at the African Nations Cup in 2002. Having toyed with the idea of playing in vests, they decided play in a one-piece strip combining shirts and shorts. FIFA promptly fined them £90,000 and deducted six points from their World Cup campaign, effectively meaning the Cameroon team could kiss goodbye to playing in the World Cup finals.

A couple of seasons later, FIFA fined Spain £45,000 for racist chanting during a game against England.

Let's get this straight. A £90,000 fine and effectively an end to your World Cup campaign for wearing the wrong kit. A £45,000 fine for racism. It would appear FIFA regard racism as a lesser offence than wearing incorrect kit.

Of course it was Sepp Blatter, the FIFA president, who advised female footballers to wear tighter and skimpier kit. Disappointment – but no surprise there, then.

25. SEEING GREY

The mid-nineties saw Manchester United play some away games in grey. Three-nil down against Southampton at halftime, Alex Ferguson knew the problem and acted immediately. No, not a change in formation or tactics but a change of kit. It was the grey kit that was entirely to blame for the three-goal deficit. Ferguson claimed that his players couldn't pick each other out against the backdrop of the compact Dell stadium.

The kit change (to blue and white) did work to a degree. They won the second half 1–0 for a moral victory.

And before you scoff, United played five games in grey and lost all five games. The Southampton game was the last time the grey kit made an appearance, although the shirts could be bought for a reduced price. I'm guessing not many were sold. You're still scoffing, aren't you?

26. NAME THAT TUNE

Football clubs take to the pitch to a wide range of tunes, some entirely appropriate, others less so.

In the early 1990s, Oldham Athletic used to raise the atmosphere to fever pitch, inspire their supporters and motivate their players by entering the gladiatorial arena to ... *'Mouldy Old Dough'*, the seventies' hit by Lieutenant Pigeon.

There are some classics of course. Name the club and the song immediately comes to mind. Liverpool? Correct, it is *'You'll Never Walk Alone'*. West Ham? Right again, *'I'm Forever Blowing Bubbles'*. Leyton Orient? Correct, Herb Alpert's *'Tijuana Taxi'*. What do you mean, you didn't know the last one?

Okay, I'll accept some teams do have rather bizarre choices. Stoke had the Tom Jones' hit *'Delilah'*, and Tranmere Rovers the theme from the *Rockford Files*. Elvis fans will be pleased to hear that Arsenal have used *'Can't Help Falling in Love with You'*, and Preston North End had *'The Wonder of You'*. Fans of punk rock and Scunthorpe United are catered for by the Irons running out to Sham 69's *'If the Kids are United'*.

First prize, though, goes to Greenbank Under-10 B Team. Their sponsor in 2006 was...? Oh come on, it's easy. Yes, that's right. Motorhead. Believe it or not the rock band sponsored the kids' team and they even ran out to *'The Ace of Spades'*.

As far as I am aware, no one takes the field to Judy Collins singing *'Send in the Clowns'*, but I'm sure that plenty should.

27. LIVING THE DREAM

Colne is the sort of place few people outside of Lancashire will have heard of. It's only real claim to fame is that the bandmaster on the *Titanic* was born there and has a memorial in his honour.

But, for a few brief years in the late 1980s and early 1990s, Colne's profile rose to unimaginable heights through the medium of non-league football.

Local business man Graham White, imaginatively nicknamed Chalky, financed a meteoric rise up the football pyramid. In the 1970s the Dynamoes played in the lowly Lancashire Combination. By 1988, they had won the FA Vase at Wembley (the equivalent of the FA Cup for teams on the lowest rungs of the football pyramid. Emley, 1–0, since you ask), by 1989 the Northern Premier Division 1 and by 1990 the Premier Division. In some ways they were the Manchester City of their day, albeit on a much, much smaller budget. But they were different: a club prepared to take on the big boys and strike a victory for small-town clubs everywhere.

Then it all went wrong. Promotion to the Conference, one step away from the Football League, was denied. The major problem was the Holt House Ground. It was okay for the Northern Premier Division, but not for the Conference. The main stand was too small and the huge slope was deemed unacceptable. It would seem that no one had thought to check out if the facilities at Colne would meet the required standard for promotion to the top of the non-league tree.

Attempts to ground share with Burnley or Blackburn came to nothing. There was also the suggestion that Chalky White had become disenchanted with the barriers being placed in the way of the club. Dynamoes folded, and the dream came to an end.

31

So, for a few years the small town of Colne had football as its claim to fame as well as the music on the *Titanic*, which went down quite well.

28. FESTIVE FUN

The new year of 1962 was anything but a happy one for football fans. That was the winter of the Big Freeze, when nearly all the matches between Boxing Day and March were postponed.

The Boxing Day fixtures in 1963 left some clubs wishing that the weather was once again the winner. That was the day the then First Division, now Premiership, went wild with an amazing 66 goals being scored in ten matches. An average of nearly seven goals a game. I'm not suggesting for a minute that some players had overdone the Christmas Day celebrations but...

HOME		AWAY	
BLACKPOOL	1	CHELSEA	5
BURNLEY	6	MAN. UNITED	1
FULHAM	10	IPSWICH	1
LEICESTER CITY	2	EVERTON	0
LIVERPOOL	6	STOKE	1
NOTTINGHAM FOREST	3	SHEFFIELD UNITED	3
WBA	4	SPURS	4
SHEFFIELD WEDNESDAY	3	BOLTON	0
WOLVES	3	ASTON VILLA	3
WEST HAM	2	BLACKBURN	8

A dull game at Leicester.

Bizarrely, two days later Manchester United beat Burnley 5–1 at Old Trafford. No doubt those from Turf Moor still claim that they won 7–6 on aggregate.

29. FOOTBALLING FALLOUTS

John Beck managed Cambridge United in the early 1990s and, using Route One Football, took them on an amazing run of successive promotions. From what was the Fourth Division they went straight through the Third and then to the play-offs in the Second for a place in the top tier of English football – before losing to Leicester City in the semi-finals.

Beck resorted to unorthodox tactics during his time at Cambridge, including making his players take a shower. Nothing unorthodox there, I hear you say – but these showers took place *before* the game. And the showers were cold. But that is nothing compared to having fight with one of your key players.

Cambridge were in second place in the old Second Division, battling for promotion to the inaugural Premier League, when Beck and star striker Steve Claridge sorted out a half-time dispute with a full-blown boxing match. The substitution of Claridge after just 20 minutes may have had something to do with this.

Beck transferred Claridge to Luton Town the following week for £120,000. Cambridge then missed out on promotion to the first Premier League and the riches that would have followed.

What happened next? Claridge was back at Cambridge five months later, bought from cash-strapped Luton for £190,000. By then, Beck had been sacked following a poor start to the season that saw Cambridge eventually relegated. They then went on a downward spiral to eventual relegation out of the Football League.

So close but yet so far.

30. SUPER MAC

Southampton has always seemed a nice, family-orientated club, especially under the guidance of genial giant and Saints legend Lawrie McMenemy. They even beat Manchester United to win the FA Cup.

A few seasons after their Wembley heroics, furious at a poor display from his central defender ginger-haired/bald-headed (depending on which bit of his footballing career you remember him from) Mark Wright, McMenemy tore into his star player in the dressing room after the game.

I suppose Wright could have acknowledged a below-par performance to the gaffer, but he didn't. Instead he pushed his boss into the showers, where both men proceeded to knock the living daylights out of each other until pulled apart by team mates. It is important to point out that they both had their clothes on. Best not to think about the alternative.

Wright was transferred to Derby County and then had to play on the bog of a pitch at the Baseball Ground, with the disgraced businessman Robert Maxwell as chairman.

31. GRIMSBY'S ITALIAN SUPERSTAR

When the former Sampdoria player Ivano Bonetti signed for Grimsby in 1995 from Serie A, it brought massive international attention to the club and he became an instant hero. The fee was £100,000. Half of this was raised by the fans and £50,000 came from Bonetti himself, further increasing his appeal.

Sadly, Mariners boss Brian Laws didn't share the love for the ageing Italian, and reacted to a 3–2 defeat at Luton in 1996 by accusing Bonetti of interrupting him during a post-match debrief. Then Laws threw a plate of food at him. Bonetti didn't have time to duck and took the flying plate in his face, sustaining a fractured cheekbone.

At the end of the season Bonetti left for Tranmere on a free transfer and Laws became manager at Scunthorpe. I'm not sure there were any winners there.

32. AVAILABILITY

The bottom line for professional footballers is the need to be available for matches. You're not much use if you can't play. Some players will have a good excuse for being unavailable, such as injury. Some will have a poor excuse, like suspension. Others will have an even poorer excuse, like being in prison.

In the 1980s, Liverpool midfielder Jan Molby was caught driving on the wrong side of the road. In a 30mph zone. At over 100mph. After speeding through a red light and – this will not come as a huge surprise – being over the limit. On the down side, he spent six weeks in jail; on the up side, the burly Dane, who would have been a 'before' in a diet campaign, claimed it helped him lose four stone.

The infamous Arsenal Tuesday Club was a cover for those in the team who wanted to over-indulge prior to their day off on a Wednesday. Members included Perry Groves and Paul Merson, but perhaps the best-known and most enthusiastic participant was Tony Adams. Back in 1990, when he was seen as a donkey rather than the footballing legend he turned out to be, Adams drove into a wall while drunk and was sentenced to four months in jail. Party pooper Arsene Wenger soon put a stop to the Tuesday Club when he arrived as manager.

Before his professional days Ian Wright, another Arsenal legend, had two weeks at Her Majesty's pleasure for having two cars. To be clear, having two cars is okay; no law broken there. It was the lack of tax and insurance that was the problem.

33. KEEPING COUNT

The most exciting bit of a cold December midweek Wigan against Bristol Rovers first half, other than a goal for the home side in the twentieth minute, was without a shadow of any doubt the few minutes of injury time. Many of the 2,800 crowd would have already joined the queues for the pies and hot drinks and missed what followed.

Bristol defender David Pritchard was sent off following a second yellow card. Before the free kick could be taken, Jason Perry and Andy Tillson followed their teammate off the pitch to demonstrate some sort of misplaced red-card solidarity. Not wanting to miss out on the red-card carnage, Wigan's Graeme Jones was also sent off. Midway through the second half, Bristol Rovers' midfielder Josh Low also picked up a red card.

Just in case you have lost count – and I wouldn't blame you – Wigan finished the game with ten players and Bristol with seven. Until Low's dismissal there had been no further goals, but what sort of formation do you play with just six outfield players? Well, one that allowed David Lowe (no relation to Josh, different spelling) to score twice and secure a 3–0 victory.

The return game in April was a much more pleasant affair, at least for Bristol who won 5–0 and made it to the play-offs on goal difference. Mid-table mediocrity had to suffice for Wigan.

Revenge is a dish best served cold.

34. MY COUSIN, THE PRESIDENT

George Weah is a Liberian politician who became president of his country. He was a former professional footballer who won numerous awards, including FIFA World Player of the Year, African Footballer of the Year on three occasions, UEFA Champions League Top Scorer and the Ballon d'Or. In short, Weah is a footballing legend and national hero.

His cousin, Ali Dia, is also known in footballing circles but for all the wrong reasons. Perhaps the most important reason is that he wasn't actually George Weah's cousin.

Gillingham, Port Vale and even West Ham supposedly had approaches from George Weah extolling the virtues of Ali Dia before Southampton signed him on trial. They were no doubt impressed by the Weah recommendation, Dia's five goals in thirteen appearances for Senegal, as well as his time spent playing at Paris Saint-Germain. Only, as Southampton were about to find out in the most public and embarrassing of circumstances, none of this was true.

Despite not being impressive in training, a glut of injuries forced manager Graeme Souness to put Dia on the bench for the home game with Leeds United. And then the unthinkable happened: Southampton legend, Matt Le Tissier, was injured and Dia came on for his one and only league appearance. In a woeful performance, described by Le Tissier as 'Bambi on ice' and positionally clueless, Souness had to substitute his substitute.

Dia turned up the following day for treatment and then was never seen again at Southampton. He just disappeared. Actually, he went on to play several times for Gateshead and scored twice but, with no disrespect to the Heed (Gateshead's nickname), it's hardly the Premier League.

35. GOURMET CATERING

The *Daily Mirror* used a Freedom of Information request to access food hygiene reports for all of the top 92 clubs in 2015. The vast majority of clubs got the top five out of five rating, but one lower league club (Mansfield Town, you know who we mean) scored a derisory one out of five. On reinspection the rating was moved to four and subsequently to the top of the hygiene league with a five. The list of concerns included having raw and cooked meat in the same fridge, a concern the club described as an isolated incident.

Another two (Yeovil, and Dagenham & Redbridge, since you asked) were sent to the naughty step (two out of five). Concerns at Yeovil related to having a dirty wall, floor, oven, meat slicer and freezer in their kitchen, which is quite a litany of failure. I can only imagine they didn't get a rock bottom one because staff wiped their feet on the way out of the kitchen. In fairness to Yeovil, they now are classed as good. That's for food hygiene, not performances on the pitch.

And before you think that these problems are reserved for the smaller clubs, the *Mirror* also ran a headline about one of the big teams from the North West (not City, the other one) being warned by food hygiene inspectors to tackle mice infestations.

Tuck in everyone and enjoy your half-time snack.

36. SEEING RED

It had all the makings of an unremarkable game in the third tier when Chesterfield played Plymouth Argyle. Chesterfield were in the middle of an FA Cup run which eventually took them to a semi-final defeat against Middlesbrough and could be excused for having their mind on the bigger games to come. A fairly innocuous and goalless first half passed with perhaps the only thing of note being the sending off of one Argyle player. In the second half Chesterfield, probably with an eye on the road to Wembley, conceded two goals. The Spireites managed to pull one back with five minutes to go, setting up a grand finale. Only it wasn't that grand

In the 88th minute Chesterfield had a corner and, in a desperate attempt to get a point from a seemingly lost cause, launched the ball into a packed penalty area. A mêlée ensued, fists were thrown and all 20 outfield players got dragged into a mass brawl. Four more players, an equal two from each team, were sent off, meaning that Chesterfield won the players on the pitch award 9–8, but lost the actual game 2–1.

Such was the ferocity and brutality of the violence that the referee later admitted to being frightened. It was the first time that five players had been sent off in a football league match.

Special mention to the Plymouth Argyle keeper. The fighting started when, having gone to catch the ball from the incoming corner, he had been elbowed and left prostrate on the floor suffering from concussion. The goalie's name might ring a few bells: step forward Bruce Grobbelaar. Or only don't step forward as you are unconscious on the floor.

But Saltergate, the venue of the debacle, obviously isn't Argentina. Probably not on the radar of many people was the Argentinian lower-league fixture featuring Claypole and Victoriano Arenas. Thirty-six red cards. Every single player and 14 subs. It probably doesn't come as a shock that the referee abandoned the game.

37. DO YOU WANT A BET?

Jimmy Gauld may not be a player recognised by many followers of football nowadays. Unfortunately, many of those who do remember him will do so for all the wrong reasons. Over a sustained period, Gauld enticed other players to gamble on the results of fixed games.

Gauld had a long and, at times, nomadic career. During his playing days there had been a whiff of scandal surrounding some games he had been involved in, but nothing was proven. By the 1962–63 season, Gauld's playing days had come to an end because of a broken leg. He then used his time and the contacts made during his footballing career to fix results. One successful ploy saw Sheffield Wednesday players David Layne, Peter Swann and Tony Kay bet on their own team losing a match against Ipswich. Two other matches that day had Gauld's fingerprints all over them. Lincoln lost to Brentford, and Oldham beat York in what emerged as a successful accumulator bet.

More players and more clubs were dragged into Gauld's gambling scheme. The following season, a Sunday newspaper exposed the exploits of the syndicate; bizarrely, Gauld sold his story for a not-inconsiderable sum of £7,000 (worth about £125,000 nowadays) to that same newspaper.

Gauld's very public confession, coupled with other evidence, resulted in him receiving a four-year prison sentence. Ten other players received sentences ranging from four months to 15 months. Life bans from the Football Association soon followed.

It was a high price to pay but, as German philosopher Friedrich Hegel once said, 'The one thing we learn from history is that we learn nothing from history.' In 2016, Joey Barton was charged with placing 1,260 bets over a ten-year period. He was banned from football for 18 months, effectively ending his playing career.

Going back to the Sheffield Wednesday game, remember Tony Kay who bet against his own team? He won the man of the match award. A very accomplished trickster, downright lucky or a man having second thoughts during the actual game?

38. MEET MY NEW TEAM

You don't get to swap and change the team you support. It's something you stick with through thick and thin and, as a Blackpool supporter, I can tell you there is often a lot of thin.

You certainly never, ever forget which team you support. Just imagine forgetting which team you support. You'd have to be a complete idiot to do that, wouldn't you? It's surely burned into your soul. Unless you are the Prime Minister, of course.

Avid (and it will become clear that this word is used in the loosest sense) Aston Villa super fan David Cameron declared his absolute allegiance to West Ham United when electioneering. He subsequently used the excuse that he got mixed up because West Ham play in the same colour kit as Villa. Taking this to its logical outcome, Mr Cameron could also support Burnley, Northampton Town, Heart of Midlothian and Stenhousemuir – although I'm not sure how many supporters would want to be associated with the ex-Prime Minister as a fellow fan.

So, at best David Cameron forgot the name of the football team he supported. At worst, he maybe, just maybe, never really supported them in the first place. I know: a politician who lied. Unthinkable!

39. NARROW MINDED

Okay, pay attention at the back. You'll need to stick with me on this one.

FIFA's rules stipulate that a football pitch should be between 90 and 120 metres in length and 45 and 90 metres in width. For UEFA matches, such as big European Cup games, the pitch must measure 105 by 69 metres. Now park this new knowledge because you will need it later.

Dynamo Kiev headed to Ibrox and Glasgow Rangers for a European Cup, second-leg fixture in 1987 holding a 1–0 lead. They were no doubt full of confidence that their expansive style of play using two wingers deployed to spread the game wide would prevail once more.

As is protocol, the Ukraine side trained on the Ibrox pitch on the day before the match and then returned to their hotel. Between then and the kick-off, Rangers reduced the width of the pitch to the absolute legal minimum and went on to win the match 2–0 and the tie 2-1 on aggregate. Kiev described the tactic as 'un-British' although Rangers probably weren't too bothered as the end justified the means.

There is a footnote to Ranger's tactical genius/devious skulduggery (delete as appropriate). Some people have very long memories. Nearly 30 years later, Alloa Athletic reduced the width of their pitch against (and I'm sure you can guess who) Rangers. Mark Warburton, who by then was the manager at Rangers, took umbrage and launched a verbal volley at the Clackmannanshire side. It fell to the Alloa chairman to remind the Glasgow Rangers' manager that it was his club that had previously come up with this ploy.

Unfortunately for the Alloa chairman, his team lost 5–1. Revenge of sorts was sweet when, in the penultimate game of the season, they played out a 1–1 draw in front of 50,000 at Ibrox.

It would appear that size does matter after all.

40. EASY AS ONE, TWO, THREE

Booking a player equals a yellow card. Booking the same player again equals two yellow cards. Two yellow cards in the same game equals one red card. It's not rocket science.

Referee Graham Poll was, we would all hope, familiar with this rule. After all, he was a referee and before that an assistant referee for more than 20 years. Only, in the 2006 Croatia v Australia World Cup group game he (eventually) sent off Josip Simunic, the Australian-born Croatian defender, for a third yellow.

This wasn't his first major mistake in a major match. Several years earlier, when he was in charge of the Everton v Liverpool derby, the clock had ticked past 90 minutes into time that Graham had added on. Sander Westervald, the Liverpool keeper, booted a free kick from just outside his area. The powerfully hit kick didn't go very far and ricocheted off his own player, Don Hutchison, back in to the empty goal. One-nil to Everton with barely seconds left. Only not. Poll disallowed it, claiming he had blown for full time before the ball crossed the line. Television pictures showed this was not the case.

Graham Poll did admit to his mistake, but only seven years later after he had retired. I might be being a bit curmudgeonly here – but not much use, then.

41. THE LUCK OF THE IRISH

Prior to every game he played, the Republic of Ireland goalkeeper Shay Given placed a bottle of Lourdes' holy water at the back of his goal as a lucky charm. Many Catholics believe water from Lourdes, where apparitions of the Virgin Mary have appeared, helps to improve their wellbeing.

We can only guess that Given forgot to pack the holy water or the Virgin Mary was on her holidays when the Republic played (I use this term loosely) in the 2012 European Championships. Played three, lost three, goals for one, goals against nine.

Only one sort of luck there, and it wasn't good.

42. TRAIN HARD, PLAY HARD

Train hard and play hard is one of those inspirational slogans used to motivate teams. Unfortunately, some players misunderstand the meaning and assume the play hard bit relates to off-the-pitch activities as opposed to on it.

Poor Graham Taylor. Not only did he have to endure the ignominy of being labelled a turnip by a tabloid newspaper after failing to get England to the 1994 World Cup finals, he also had to manage Paul Gascoigne and Paul McGrath. Fortunately, not at the same time.

Paul Gascoigne's descent into alcoholism is well documented and so very sad. At the time the then England manager, Graham Taylor, suggested Gazza had 'refuelling problems'. In a later interview, Taylor said that if he had come straight out and said that the Geordie was an alcoholic just imagine what the headlines would have been.

In his excellent autobiography *Back from the Brink*, McGrath writes of his respect for Taylor who was quick to realise he not only had a player with dodgy knees but also chronic alcohol problems. Taylor used all his man-management skills to coax the best out of the wayward Irishman who, in addition to regularly being crowned Villa's top player, was elected as player of the season by his fellow professionals.

Of course, there are many other players who due to alcohol have failed to understand the word 'professional' in the term 'professional footballer'.

43. CAN I HAVE MY SHIRT BACK PLEASE?

Footballing legend Pele once gave away his football shirt to a fan; it is the sort of gesture popular throughout world football, and the sort of gesture that made Pele in particular popular throughout the world.

It was only after a run of not scoring that Pele decided he wanted his 'lucky shirt' back. An associate was dispatched to find the fan and secure its safe return. Several days later the associate was able to return the top to Pele, who promptly picked up where he had left off with his goal scoring.

What Pele didn't know is that the fan hadn't been located and the associate had passed on a used shirt he had found in the changing rooms.

44. SPITTING IMAGE

As part of his pre-match preparation, David James of Watford, Liverpool, Aston Villa, West Ham United, Manchester City, Portsmouth, Bristol City, Bournemouth, ÍBV Vestmannaeyjar, Kerala Blasters and *Strictly Come Dancing* fame used to spit on urinal walls before games. He also considered it unlucky for someone to touch his gloves.

He used to go through 24-hour rituals before a game, which involved eating, showering and sleeping at exactly the same time as he had before the previous match.

Did this serial superstition work? A clue might be in his nickname, Calamity James.

45. POST-MATCH EXCUSES

The story goes that Arsenal will never let their goalkeeper wear a brand-new shirt unless it has already been washed. Apparently, this dates back to the Gunners 1927 FA Cup Final defeat to Cardiff, when keeper Dan Lewis blamed a greasy new top for the mistake that led to the only goal of the game. Well, he would, wouldn't he?

With the great Herbert Chapman as manager and a very talented team, it would only be a matter of time before the Gunners were back at Wembley to claim their first FA Cup win. Three years, in fact, when they beat Huddersfield. Unfortunately, Dan wasn't back. He was injured and didn't play.

Within a year that injury had forced him out of the game. He did have three appearances for Wales to look back on in retirement. Regrettably, his third and final international was a 6–0 defeat to England.

A bit like his FA Cup final appearance, it was probably not a match Dan would want to remember.

46. WE ARE GOING UP, THEN BACK DOWN

Back in the Premier League after a five-year absence, the 2007–08 season promised so much for Derby County supporters. Their return came via a Wembley win in the play-off finals against West Bromwich Albion. After five minutes of the first game on their Premier League return, their euphoric fans were chanting 'We are top of the league' when they took a 1–0 lead against Portsmouth before securing a late draw.

It is probably fair to say it was all downhill from then on. After four more games (won nil, drawn zero, lost four, one goal for, 13 against), at the start of September a well-known bookmaker payed out on bets that Derby would be relegated. They went on to win just one game in the league all season (Newcastle United, hang your heads in shame) and set a top-flight record of going 32 league games without a win. To be fair to Derby, they were able to celebrate one other win by beating Championship side Sheffield Wednesday in the FA Cup. Having said that, they needed a replay and penalties to do so.

There was some comfort for fans of the Rams. They were not the only team to have gone through a season in the top division with only one win. Loughborough also achieved this feat in 1899–1900.

On reflection, I'm not sure this would have offered any comfort to Derby supporters.

47. MANCHESTER CITY WERE RUBBISH

Younger readers may find this hard to believe, but there was a time not too long ago when Manchester City were rubbish. And I mean really, really rubbish.

Relegated from the top flight to the second tier in 1983, promoted back to the top flight in 1985, relegated again in 1987, promoted back again in 1989. Then, after several seasons best described as average, it got worse. In 1996 they were relegated from the Premiership. Two years later City were relegated again, and were in the third tier of English football.

The derby game that season wasn't at Old Trafford but at Moss Road, home of Macclesfield Town, with an attendance of just over 6,000. Back-to-back promotions brought City a Lazarus-like return to the Premier Division – but then they relegated again straight away. Of course, by now they were used to this and bounced back immediately. In the eight seasons between 1996 and 2003 the played in seven different divisions!

More recently, it's all been a bit different. But diehard fans can still remember the euphoria on September 12th 1998 when Manchester City triumphed 1–0 at the mighty Macclesfield, thanks to a goal after 86 minutes.

How times have changed.

48. EVERYONE'S A WINNER

It was Irish playwright George Bernard Shaw who said, 'England and America are two countries separated by a common language.'

This might go some way towards explaining the American attitude to relegation. They don't do it; in America, you can never be relegated. Alexi Lalas, the ex-general manager at LA Galaxy where David Beckham spent some of his time playing, has said that relegation is a very foreign concept to sports in the United States. Football is a business; if you want to attract investment, you need to make sure that when you join a league you stay in that league.

So, don't leave anything to chance or ability and do away with relegation. Nobody is the ultimate loser. No relegation or promotion battles, no last day scraps to stay up.

D, U, double L. Dull.

49. YOU DON'T KNOW WHAT YOU'RE DOING! OR DO YOU?

After retiring from a lengthy playing career, England centre-half Terry Fenwick looked to stay in football as a manager. True, his playing career hadn't been all wine and roses – actually, a lot of it had possibly been wine as he was given a four-month prison sentence for drink-driving.

His first managerial post saw him take up the hot seat at Portsmouth. After three not particularly successful seasons, he was sacked. A few years of non-league wilderness followed with little success before Northampton Town came to his rescue – only he didn't come to theirs. The Cobblers, with Fenwick as manager, started the 2003 season with seven winless league games before someone worked up the courage to tell him he had overstayed his welcome.

More non-league appointments followed before he became manager at (and I'm not sure you are going to believe this but I promise you it is true) San Juan Jabloteh in the Trinidad and Tobago Pro League. His record there was actually quite good, winning the league on four occasions.

Although no longer managing, he still coaches in his adopted Caribbean home. I somehow think Terry is having the last laugh.

50. NORWAY AWAY

In the build-up to their World Cup Qualifier against Norway, England must have been supremely confident. Okay, it was away in Oslo but England had never scored less than four goals in a game against the Nordic minnows. After 16 minutes, a Bryan Robson goal saw them set fair for the usual triumph, only someone forgot to tell the Norwegians that they were supposed to give up at this point and leak goals. They won 2–1. And, much to England's embarrassment, one of the best bits of football commentary was unleashed...

'...and he adds time and he adds time. The English are about to lose to ... that's the whistle! That's the whistle! Norway have defeated England 2–1! We are the world's best! We are the world's best! We have defeated England 2–1! It is incredible! We have defeated England! Eng-land, home of the giants! Lord Nelson! Lord Beaverbrook! Sir Winston Churchill! Sir Anthony Eden! Clement Attlee! Henry Cooper! Lady Diana! We have beaten each and every one of you! Maggie Thatcher, can you hear me? I have a message for you. I have a message for you right in the middle of your election campaign: we have sent England out of the World Cup! Maggie Thatcher! As they say in the boxing bars around Madison Square Garden in New York in your own language: Your boys took a hell of a beating! Your boys took a hell of a beating! Because, Maggie Thatcher, Norway have defeated England! We are the world's best'

Norwegian commentator Bjørge Lillelien, take a bow.

I don't want to spoil the romance here, but I will. Despite this glorious win, Norway ended up last in the qualifying group and England still went through to the World Cup finals.

Printed in Great Britain
by Amazon

51657319R00036